Real Estate Investing

Comprehensive Beginner's Guide for Newbies

Michael McCord

Copyright 2016- Michael McCord- All rights reserved.

This document is geared towards providing exact and reliable information in regards to the topic and issue covered. The publication is sold with the idea that the publisher is not required to render accounting, officially permitted, or otherwise, qualified services. If advice is necessary, legal or professional, a practiced individual in the profession should be ordered.

- From a Declaration of Principles which was accepted and approved equally by a Committee of the American Bar Association and a Committee of Publishers and Associations.

In no way is it legal to reproduce, duplicate, or transmit any part of this document in either electronic means or in printed format. Recording of this publication is strictly prohibited and any storage of this document is not allowed unless with written permission from the publisher. All rights reserved.

The information provided herein is stated to be truthful and consistent, in that any liability, in terms of inattention or otherwise, by any usage or abuse of any policies, processes, or directions contained within is the solitary and utter responsibility of the recipient reader. Under no circumstances will any legal responsibility or blame be held against the publisher for any reparation, damages, or monetary loss due to the information herein, either directly or indirectly.

Respective authors own all copyrights not held by the publisher.

Table of Contents

Introduction 1

Chapter 1: Why Real Estate? 5

Chapter 2: Make the Most of Your Real Estate Investments 11

Chapter 3: Avoid These Common Mistakes 17

Chapter 4: Invest in Residential Rental Property 23

Chapter 5: Invest in Turnkey Rental Properties 29

Chapter 6: Invest in REITs 35

Chapter 7: Invest in Properties to Flip 41

Chapter 8: Staging a Home for Resale 47

Chapter 9: Invest in Properties to Wholesale 55

Conclusion 61

Introduction

Congratulations on purchasing *Real Estate Investing: Comprehensive Beginner's Guide for Newbies* and thank you for doing so. Investing in real estate is a surefire way to create long term income streams as long as you go about doing it in the right manner.

BONUS:
Revolutionary Credit Repair Secrets

And as a special thank you to my readers, I am giving away free copies of my book- **Revolutionary Credit Repair Secrets- Cardinal Rules to Get You a Perfect Credit Score.** You will receive outstanding tips to improve your credit score, which will assist you both in Real Estate Investing and in other financial health matters.

To get instant access to this book and more awesome resources, check out the link below:

https://mccordpublishing.leadpages.co/real-estate-investing

As an added bonus, subscribers will be given a chance to get exclusive sneak peeks of upcoming books and discounts that will not be available to the general public. You will also have the opportunity to obtain free copies of my books with no strings attached. Don't worry, we treat your e-mail with the respect it deserves. We will not spam you and that's a promise!

What We Will Cover on Real Estate Investing:

To help ensure that you end up with more amazing properties than you do lemons, the following chapters will outline the concepts that make real estate investment such a good choice before discussing tips for ensuring you maximize every real estate investment while avoiding common pitfalls. You will then learn a step by step approach to successfully finding, purchasing and renting out property, the basics of investing in an REIT, how to find the best properties to flip for a profit and how to make money without fixing up a thing via wholesaling property. While the tips and methods outlined below will make investing in real estate much more manageable, it is important that you keep in mind it will take time for you to start seeing results. Keep at it, however, and you will be turning a profit before you know it.

Additionally, the art of Real Estate Investing is a complex topic and has many components. Our books tackle these other components such as **Flipping Houses for Profit, Rental Property Investing,** how to become a **Real Estate Agent**, and even a step by step guide to achieving an **excellent Credit Score** to get you the loan with the best rates. And for anyone interested in the **Tiny House Movement**, we have books on that subject as well!!

Please check out our Amazon Author Page to find selections like this!

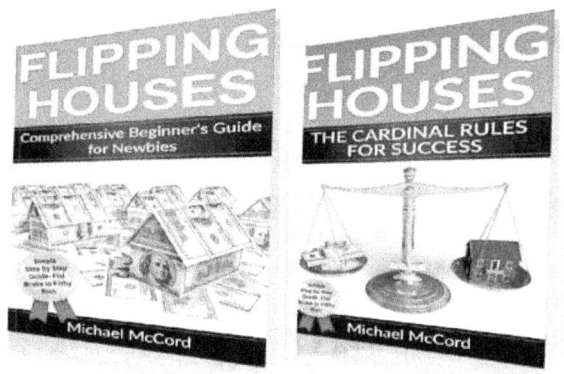

https://www.amazon.com/Flipping-Houses-Comprehensive-Beginners-Properties-ebook/dp/B01MQCR3OP

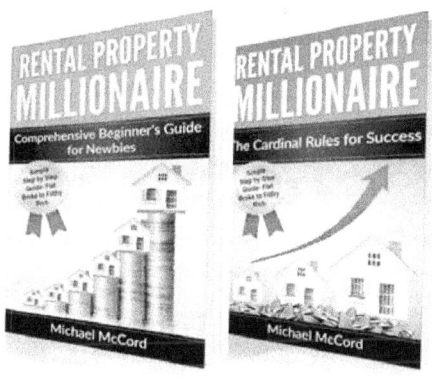

https://www.amazon.com/Rental-Property-Investing-Comprehensive-Investment-ebook/dp/B01M69Y22J

Michael McCord

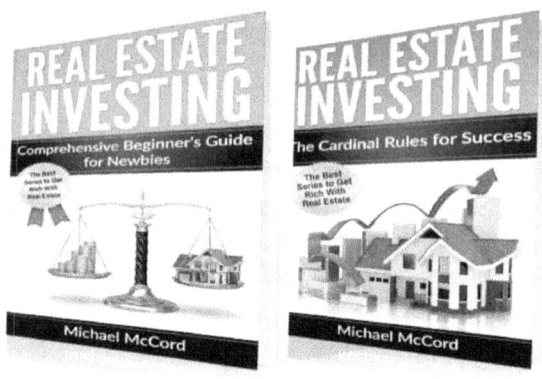

https://www.amazon.com/Michael-McCord/e/B01LYIFPLO/

https://www.amazon.com/Michael-McCord/e/B01LYIFPLO/

There are plenty of books on this subject on the market, thanks again for choosing this one! Every effort was made to ensure it is full of as much useful information as possible, please enjoy!

Chapter 1:
Why Real Estate?

When it comes to investment opportunities, both passive and active, there is no older form of investment than real estate investment, a form of it having been practiced since humanity first discovered the idea of property ownership. More importantly, it is one of a handful of asset types that every serious investor should consider eventually, be it when they are first starting out or are simply looking to strengthen and diversify their portfolio. The fact that it offers benefits related to profitability, net worth, diversification, cash flow and liquidity all mean that it is a good idea to get your first real estate investment off the ground sooner rather than later.

While understanding the benefits related to real estate investment is fairly basic, learning to put them to use effectively can be more difficult than many people expect, but only if you commit to doing so unprepared. To prevent this from happening, this chapter will outline the basic principles at work in real estate investment, the various types of real estate investment you can consider and the potential risks and rewards of each.

Real estate investment basics

At its most basic, investing in real estate is the act of profiting from holdings related to physical property regardless if the specifics include selling, investing or operating it. The most common form of real estate investment that most people are familiar with is purchasing a property to rent out to others at a set rate for a specific period of time, though it is far from the only type. Regardless, it remains popular among those who enjoy having their investments seem tangible as compared to more ethereal investments such as those made in the forex market. If the idea of walking through your investment appeals to you, then real estate might be for you.

There are four primary ways that real estate investors can make money on their investments. First and most reliably, is what is known as appreciation. Appreciation is the process by which natural changes in the real estate market over time result in an increased value for a given property irrespective of the actions taken by that property's owner. Appreciation can then be accelerated based on things like a shortage of property in a given area of changes and improvements that an owner makes to a property. While appreciation can amount to a significant return over time, you do not want to make investments that seem as though they would be a good idea based solely on what you expect to happen with its appreciation rates. Think of appreciation as the cherry on top of the real estate investment sundae.

Instead you are going to want to focus on generating a steady cash flow with the real estate that you purchase which means actively doing something with the property that you purchase. First and foremost, it is important to understand that property doesn't need to just mean things like houses or condominiums, it also means things like car washes, storage units, even office buildings or hotels. Real estate investments are all around you, you just need to focus on seeing them in the right light. Furthermore, depending on the various types of real estate investments that you do end up moving forward on, you can then also count on further ancillary income based on things like vending machines or washers and dryers in apartment complexes or hotels. While this type of income is likely not going to be reliable enough to live off of, it will add up substantially over time. When it comes to planning out your real estate investment it is important to keep in mind that there are plenty of different ways to pay for the properties you are thinking about purchasing, even if you don't have the cash or the credit score to go about it via the most traditional of means. If you plan on taking out a loan then you are going to want to generate leverage, which in this case means using someone else's money to purchase the property at a price you can still make a profit on it. This can be a risky move, depending on your level or real estate competence, but the rewards can also be substantial.

Regardless of what your ultimate plan turns out to be, it is important that you get started on the right foot by forming a Limited Liability Company that will technically be in charge of all of your real estate holdings. This is a crucial step as otherwise, if something terrible were to happen to someone else on one of your properties they could sue you directly and potentially take everything you have in the process. With an LLC in place, the worst that could happen is that you have to shutter the company and disband the LLC. Setting up an LLC can be done online in minutes, for less than $300. A good rule for investing is to always hope for the best but still plan for the worst, this is good advice in general and particularly important in this instance.

Real estate investment options

Rentals: If you take your time when it comes to finding the right property so that you can make a profit on the lease agreement, assuming the property stays occupied of course, then it is not unreasonable to expect as much as a 7 percent return on your initial investment each year which is about what you can expect if you play the stock market successfully or own a business that can turn a profit, though it is considered a less risky investment than either of those. Rental properties can also be a great form of passive income, assuming you go into the process with that course of action in mind so that you can account for property management fees in the rental price.

This in no way means that rental properties aren't with a certain degree of risk as well, however, as the 00s proved that the housing market is in no way unassailable. As such, especially if you are planning on buying a rental property using credit, you will want to be very sure of the strength of the market in your area and what the true value of the property is worth compared to the rates you are paying for the loan. The best case scenario if you are using a loan is instead to wait for a period of overall inflation to be incoming which means that the money you use to pay back the loan will actually be worth less than the money you borrowed.

REITS: Real Estate Investment Trusts are the stock equivalent of real estate ownership. They were first created as a way of giving those who would otherwise never be able to purchase something major like a hotel or major office complex a way to experience the benefits of owning such things. If you are looking for a truly passive form of income when it comes to real estate investment, then REITs are for you. In this instance, you put in the time up front to find an REIT that appears as though it is going to be profitable and then occasionally check in to see what your shares are currently worth. The REIT brokerage or Roth IRA that you are working with then takes care of the rest.

In order to be classified as such, REITs are required to give away at least 90 percent of their total profits to shareholders in the form of dividends. These dividends tend to be less flexible than other types of real estate based profits for multiple reasons. First, they aren't considered qualified dividends which means that you will have to pay taxes on them even though you already paid taxes on the original income. This can be avoided, however, if the profits are put into a retirement account instead. The dividends are also only given out on a set schedule, though the price of shares of an REIT are always known so shareholders can always cash out if the money gets too good.

Flipping Houses: If you like the idea of profiting from real estate ownership but you want to do so all up front instead of over time, then flipping houses might be for you. In this type of real estate investment, you take the time to find a property that you know can be fixed up for a reasonable amount, fix it up or pay someone to do it for you, and then sell the new and improved property for a profit. While occasionally there are house flippers who do just about everything themselves, a majority are going to hire contractors to take care of the details. This type of real estate investment is highly speculative, especially early on when you don't have much experience as a property can easily grow out of control when it comes to renovations, eating up your profits in the process.

This type of real estate investment is going to require lots of research in terms of what a particular area is looking for both in terms of profitable properties and also potential buyers. You are going to need to know everything about a property from the various perks related to its location to the total estimated cost of a complete remodel and what the property is likely to be worth after the fact. Luckily, you don't need to necessarily do everything yourself, however, as all the best house flippers have a team they can count on to take care of most of the actual work. While it can be expensive, proper planning early on can ensure you still make a profit on every property you flip.

Property Wholesaling: If you like the idea of making all of your money up front but don't want to actually go to all the trouble of fixing up a property in order to do so, then property wholesaling might be the type of real estate investment for you. Property wholesaling starts off quite similar to property flipping in that you will need to do research and find a property that is in need of help that can be turned around for a profit when all is said and done. Unlike with a traditional flip, however, you will also need to factor in the price of a finder's fee. This is because you are going to get the property under contract and then sell it to someone who is then actually going to go through the trouble of flipping it.

Property wholesaling can be easier than property flipping in that you have to do less physical work, while not having to worry about hiring a fully fleshed out team as well. On the other hand, finding the right properties that you can work with is going to be much more difficult, and the profit margins are going to be much slimmer. Plus, there are legal issues surrounding property wholesaling in some states.

Chapter 2:
Make the Most of Your Real Estate Investments

While you are first learning the ropes when it comes to real estate investment, it is perfectly normal for each property you visit to fill you with worry as much as potential excitement because there is just so much to consider up front. Luckily, the following tips can be used to help you gain your footing as quickly as possible.

Know the lingo

First and foremost, if you plan on being taken seriously by those in the real estate industry or its ancillary fields, or even by other real estate investors, then you are going to want to be familiar with all of the lingo and jargon you are likely to come across on a regular basis. While asking someone to explain a term you have never heard before is always preferable to making an uninformed decision, especially when there is a significant amount of money on the line, appearing as knowledgeable as the person you are speaking with is more preferable still.

- *Adverse use:* If a property is currently being utilized by someone who does not have the property owner's express permission to do so then that property can be said to be the victim of adverse use.

- *Agreement of sale:* An agreement of sale is a document that is typically drawn up by the person who is intent on buying a property, or their representation, and sent to the seller to make it clear what the buyer's terms are in relation to the property in question.

- *Amortization:* The process of amortization can be described as breaking the total price of a property down into monthly payment chunks.

- *Back to back escrow:* If an investor is in the middle of purchasing one property while also selling another property at the same time then they are considered to be in back to back escrow.

- *Balloon payment:* If the final payment on a loan is going to be much more than the average loan payment in an effort to balance out the loan and pay it off completely then that payment is considered a balloon payment.

- *Capital gains tax:* A federal tax, the capital gains tax is the tax that you will pay on the amount that your property appreciates each year.

- *Cap rate:* Written as a percentage, the cap rate indicates an estimate of potential profits over a set period of time.

- *Closing statement:* The last document that a property buyer and seller see before the final contract is written up- the closing statement- outlines the finalized details regarding the transaction in question.

- *Days on the market:* The difference between the day the property was placed on the market and the day it sold is the number of days the property spent on the market.

- *Deed of trust:* A contract between a person interested in purchasing a property and the financial institution or private individual giving out the loan to make the purchase possible is referred to as a deed of trust. It allows the lender to take the property if the loan is not repaid.

- *Equity:* The amount that the property owner will make on a given property after all expenses are accounted for is referred to as the property's equity.

- *Examination of title:* A title company can perform a search to determine all of the previous owners of a given title. This search is referred to as an examination of title.

- *Forbearance:* If a property is in the early stages of foreclosure and the lender agrees to put the foreclosure process on hold, while also forgiving previous late payments, then that property is said to be in forbearance.

- *IRA:* The type of retirement account that you can put real estate investment profits into without penalty if the funds are withdrawn after you reach retirement age is referred to as an IRA.

- *Notice of Default:* If the property buyer ends up not repaying the loan at the rate that the lender would like, the lender sends out a notice of default to let the property owner known that they have breached the loan contract which means the foreclosure process will be starting soon.

- *Right to Recision:* After you have successfully applied for a loan, you have a set period of time to determine if you want to cancel your loan request, that period of time is known as your right to recision period.

- *Title insurance:* Title insurance protects the person who purchased it, either the buyer or the seller, in case the property in question ends up in a legal dispute.

- *Walk through:* Prior to signing the contract to purchase a property the future owner is given one last chance to look at the property before taking ownership of it, this last look is referred to as a walk through.

Be well informed

Know what you are getting into: Picking the type of real estate investment strategy that is right for you is more than picking the one that requires the least work or the one with the biggest potential for payoff and if you hope to find the one that is right for you, you are going to need to understand exactly what is going to be required of you in order to find the type of success that you are looking for. Real estate investment can be extremely reliable, but only if you put in the time and effort that is required to see it through. Additionally, you are going to want to keep in mind that investing in real estate is a skill which means that you will only improve with practice. Plan on making mistakes early on and see them as learning opportunities rather than obstacles to success.

Know enough to know your blind spots: Those who ultimately find success in real estate investment in the long term don't necessarily learn everything they can about every facet of practice, there is simply too much to learn. Instead, they focus on a few core areas related to the types of investments that they are the most interested in and then learn the basics of the rest so when they run up against something they don't know, they at least know where to go to find someone who does. In most types of real estate investment, it also pays to have sort of team on hand who you can trust to be on your side and give you straight facts when you need them. Regardless, no one is an island and nowhere is this truer than in real estate.

Be prepared: When it comes to finding the types of properties that are going to pay off in your favor, going to check out a new property blind is never the right choice. Before you set foot on a property you should already know everything you possibly can about it, including an estimate on the price based on what you have been able to see of it online. This means you are going to want to familiarize yourself with the tools that real estate investors typically use to separate the wheat from the chaff when it comes to the types of properties that you are looking for. Likewise, you are going to want to do everything you can to improve your research skills early as this will possibly save you thousands of hours in the long term. Finally, you are also going to want to ensure you become a student of the market to the point that you can hopefully predict where it is going to be moving next.

Think outside the box: If you hope to build long term wealth in the real estate investment market then you are going to need to shy away from textbook investments in favor of something a little more creative. If you take the path less traveled when it comes to real estate investment then not only will you have less competition, but the properties that you do come across will have a much greater potential for profit on average than if you were to simply look for properties online.

Always know the math: Above all else, whenever you start considering a new real estate investment the first thing you should always think about is that potential profit minus expenses equals cash flow. This means that while sometimes it will be in your best financial interests to break out the elbow grease and tackle a problem yourself, it will just as likely be cheaper in terms of man hours to hire someone to complete a task for you. Additionally, before you commit to any type of renovation or restoration you are going to want to have a good idea of what it is going to cost so you can compare it to how much you are ultimately going to make from changes in the long run. Finding the right numbers is likely going to be difficult at first, but it will get easier in the long run once you have had plenty of practice.

Chapter 3:
Avoid These Common Mistakes

When you are learning the ropes when it comes to real estate investment, having tips to point you in the right direction is nice, but it is ultimately not going to be enough on its own. Additionally, you are going to need to know about the common mistakes many new real estate investors make so that you are aware of how best to avoid them.

Never plan in the moment: Many new real estate investors wind up in the field because they first found themselves in a position when a piece of property presented itself to them for a price that appeared at first blush to be too good to pass up. In turn, they are left with a mass of new bills and no clear idea of how they are going to get everything in order. This story almost always ends in disaster which is why you never want to put yourself into a situation where you are forced to plan on the go. Planning on the go makes it impossible for you to have a true understanding of what the numbers would tell you to do with the property in question, which means that you are essentially gambling with your investment money, and there are always better ways to gamble than with real estate.

Never expect the shortest timeframe: Even wholesaling property, typically considered the fastest way to interact with property directly, can still take a month or more depending on a wide variety of factors, some of which won't be visible until after you have already made a deal with the seller. As such, when you are getting into real estate investment it is important that you understand just what you are getting yourself into, timewise, as trying to rush the process is only going to leave you wishing you had taken your time more often than not.

For example, to start you are going to want to do research on the current state of the market in general, as well as the state of things in the area you are considering purchasing property in. From there, you are going to need to research the specifics regarding the type of property you are interested in, in a chosen area so that when a good deal comes along you will be able to spot it. Then you are going to need to wait until a property comes along to make the entire thing worthwhile, hardly a quick process, especially if you are looking to wholesale the property in question. After all of that, if you are planning to take out a traditional loan in order to afford the property you hope to buy you will need to budget for at least two months in order to find out if you qualify and then one more month for everything to finally go through properly.

Likewise, you will find that going through the motions when it comes to finding someone to rent your newly purchased property or to sell it once it has been fixed up is going to take longer than you would like as well. What's more, this process can easily take much longer than it otherwise might, simply due to unexpected external factors that cropped up after you were already in the process of trying to turn a profit on the property. While there are also several factors that can align to work in your favor, the point is that making a return on real estate is never going to happen quickly. Instead, the benefits come from the fact that you will always make a profit given a long enough timeline simply because there will always be less available land tomorrow than there is today.

Don't underestimate relationships: When it comes to successfully investing in real estate it is important to keep in mind that even the most self-sufficient investor is going to need to foster a few key relationships if they hope to be effective in the long term. First and foremost, you are going to want to find a real estate agent that you can work with who you trust to find you the best deals possible. Depending on the type of investing you are doing, the right real estate agent can cut down on the amount of work you have to do personally when it comes to finding properties, and also find you better deals than you might otherwise have access to.

Furthermore, if you plan on using loans to finance the early part of your real estate investment career then you are also going to want to find a local lender with competitive rates who you can build a mutually beneficial relationship with. This should ultimately lead to better rates, which means more money in your pocket per investment property. Additionally, you are going to want a real estate lawyer you can count on, a home inspector who can be available on short notice and an appraiser you have a good relationship with. Finally, over time you will likely find a need for many other services including a cleaning service, pool service, lawn service and overall handyman. Finding quality work for a price you can live with in any of these fields is a huge win and you will want to do everything you can to nurture these types of relationships where you find them.

Don't give in to concessions too easily: The general maximum profit you can expect to see from a property is set as soon as a sale price is agreed upon between the buyer and the seller. That amount is then slowly chipped away by every product or service you require in order to turn the property around for a profit. As such, while haggling over the last thousand dollars of a property deal might not be worth the extra effort, if you use that same mentality every time you pay for a product or service to improve the property, you will quickly rack up significantly higher costs than you otherwise might. In turn, to ensure you aren't paying too much in the moment, when things absolutely need to be taken care of now, you should do yourself a favor and scout out the best prices for products you know you are going to need ahead of time.

While big box stores might not be willing to work with you on the price per item for common goods, if you find a local retailer for the products you are looking for, and make it clear that you are going to be buying in bulk when you find the right store to make it worth your while, you will be surprised at the success you can have. From there, once you have a clear idea of what certain items are going to cost, you will be able to make a more educated guess when coming up with a cost for the property as a whole and also save yourself money when it comes to purchasing last minute items as frugally as possible.

Failing to read the fine print: While the prevalence of end user license agreements for electronic interactions has made reading through the fine print of every contract a dying skill, when signing a contract for property its importance cannot be stressed enough. While having already done all the required research can make it easy to get carried away in an effort to move forward on the deal, skipping through the details can easily leave you open to clauses that were added at the last minute in a hope to profit from exactly that type of behavior. If you are unsure of your ability to make sense of everything that is being laid out, hire a real estate lawyer, the extra cost will always be worth it.

Come up with too hopeful of an estimate: Especially early on in your time as a real estate investor, it can be easy to let your emotions get the best of you when it comes to accurately estimating the cost of a given property. This can manifest itself as either overvaluing what the property is ultimately going to be worth when everything is said and done or undervaluing what the cost of various key renovations is going to be. It can even be something as simple as not taking into account various maintenance costs that will need to be paid if the property ends up sitting empty. Whatever the specifics, it is important to keep in mind that underestimates can add up quickly and before you know it your profits are practically nonexistent.

Never split your focus: While eventually you can realistically expect to move through a back to back escrow without worry, for the time being it is recommended that you only focus on a single property at once. While you will always want to be keeping an eye out for good deals that might be ready to go in the future, when it comes to actively owning and interacting with an investment property, you are going to want to ensure your focus is on the task at hand, instead of how you are going to deal with a pair of properties at a single time. Having too many irons in the fire right up front is a good way to miss something crucial and pay the price for it in a big way.

Chapter 4:
Invest in Residential Rental Property

As previously noted, investing in rental property is one of the most common ways that many people use to get started in the field. As a novice at rental property investment, you are likely going to either want to focus on a single family house, a condominium, or a small apartment complex or duplex. If you plan on using a property management company to cut down on the amount of work you will personally be doing with the property, then you are likely going to want to go with either a condominium or an apartment complex as property management companies don't often want to work with individuals with just a sole single family home in their real estate portfolio.

Find the right area

When it comes to choosing the right area for your rental property, the first thing you are going to want to do is to narrow down your search to a general area. To do this you can start by looking at the price of properties in the area in general, as well as what available properties are renting for. Once you find one or two areas that you are interested in, you will want to take a boots on the ground approach before proceeding any further. You are going to want to visit the neighborhood in question, both during the day and again at night in order to ensure things don't change too dramatically in the interim.

Once there, you are going to want to go ahead and talk to some of the locals to ensure there is nothing you are missing. When choosing who to speak with, you are going to want to avoid property owners as they have a personal stake in the area which means they are more likely to lie. Instead, your best bet is to find other renters, if there is an axe to grind with the area in question, they will tell you about it. You will also want to visit the local police station so you can get a good idea of the crime rate in the area as well.

Finally, you are going to want to consider the type of individuals that the neighborhood is likely going to attract. With this information in mind you can then more accurately determine what the amenities are like for that market as well as determine how individual properties that come up for sale might look to those individuals as well. Additionally, knowing this information will make it easier for you to keep an ear out for local news that might specifically affect the demographic in question.

Residential rental property pros and cons

Condominiums: There are several things about condominiums that naturally make them a good fit for those who are just starting to invest in real estate. For starters, they are likely to attract young, upwardly mobile renters who tend to be relatively low maintenance and also pay their bills on time. Additionally, you won't have to worry about finding a property management company as one will automatically come with the property. Finally, all the maintenance and day to day issues are all going to be handled as well, letting you sit back and collect your profits. On the down side, however, condominiums generally produce lower overall returns because the rent is lower than it would be on a single family property while also appreciating at a slower rate for the same reason.

Single family properties: Rental homes are more likely going to attract families or multiple individuals in a stronger relationship than in many other rental scenarios. This means that the overall amount of income you can rely on the renter's having is going to be higher and more stable overall. Additionally, renters who are looking for houses instead of apartment tend to be looking for something more long term as well. Tenants in these situations will require more of the property and their landlord, however, which means that it can take longer to find the right renter and it will also require more work to get the property back to a neutral state after they have gone.

Multifamily property: Whether it is a duplex or a small apartment complex, multifamily properties are typically going to generate a more reliable income stream than either of the other options simply because you have a greater group of tenants to depend on. Additionally, you can typically easily find a property management company, or even an individual to live in one of the units in question in exchange for acting as your stand-in on the premise, cutting out the cost of a property management company entirely. On the downside, you have to trust that the previous landlord rented to the right people because if not the quality of your tenants could easily be below average.

Paying for it

Once you find the right property for you, the next step is actually being able to pay for it. When it comes to getting a traditional property loan, investment properties are treated differently than primary residence, meaning that you are going to need to have at least 20 percent of the total cost of the property you want to purchase up front if you hope to have a chance. If you don't have the capital to put 20 percent down on the house, then you are likely going to need two mortgages on the property which will affect your overall profits significantly.

If you are committed to going the traditional bank route you are also going to want to have a credit score that is 740 or above and an investment plan that indicates a loan/value ratio that is realistic for the current real estate market. You will also be required to show that you are capable of handling six months of expenses if you hope to be labeled an acceptable risk.

If this doesn't sound like something that you can realistically expect to qualify for, your best option is instead going to be talking to any potential sellers that you meet about the possibility of setting up an owner financing scenario. When bank loans were a dime a dozen, asking for seller financing manifested as a big red flag for sellers. Now however, studies show that around 20 percent of all sellers are open to the prospect which means it no longer hurts to ask. You may find a seller who is agreeable to it. If it works out, what you are essentially doing is signing a promissory note say that you agree to pay a set amount of the loan the seller is giving you each month plus interest.

Fix it up

After you have found a property in an area that you like for an amount that you can afford to actually pull the trigger on, the next thing you are going to want to do is to get it ready to put on the market. When it comes to getting their first rental property ready for actual renters, it is common for new property owners to go overboard and make the property as impeccable as possible. While going all out is something that your tenants will appreciate, it isn't something that they are willing to pay extra for, however, which is why you are going to want to approach the renovations with a critical eye.

This doesn't mean that you want to leave things in a dank, dangerous or dingy fashion, but it does mean that you don't need to worry about fixing up every nook and cranny. As long as you replace the kitchen cabinets and counters and give the bathroom a bit of a makeover, lots of smaller issues will be accepted by tenants without so much as a peep. Additionally, if your budget is tight, a high likelihood if this is your first rental property, then you can easily hold off on replacing long-term systems until they give out as you are going to be responsible for the repairs or replacements regardless. Finally, when it comes to painting the property you are going to want to stick with something besides white that will work with numerous color palates.

Finding the right rental price

When it is finally time to choose what you are going to charge for the rental property that you have been working so hard on, the baseline price is going to be a combination of what other properties in the area are renting for and a price that will cover all of your bills related to the property, with a little left over for profit. From there you can then add in anything that makes your property stand out from the crowd and any other amenities that are included with the rental price.

Remember, setting the right price up front is extremely important because you will have to live with it until any lease that is signed expires. To that end, a reliable baseline to ensure you are not undervaluing your property is to keep in mind that if you paid $100,000 for a property you are going to want to get at least $1,000 back each month, if you paid $200,000 for a property then you are going to want to get at least $2,000 back each month and so on. This is called the 1 percent rule and it works for any type of property.

Chapter 5:
Invest in Turnkey Rental Properties

Another type of rental property that many first-time or younger investors like to try their hand at is a turnkey rental. The term "turnkey" describes any product, property or otherwise, that is ready for the consumer immediately after the time of purchase. When the term is used to describe real estate investments, it's meant that the investor buys, fixes up, and sells or rents the property through a third party, usually from a distance. The goal is to make the whole process as simple as possible, so all that has to be done is "turning a key".

Turnkey Companies

There are many different turnkey real estate providers all over the country, and not all of them operate the same way. Some providers will buy a property, fix it up, rent it out, and then sell it to you. However, for the purposes of this book, that's not the kind we're going to talk about. We're focused on using turnkey providers to find properties to rent. Some companies will do everything for you, while some will have you do the heavy lifting if there is rehab work that needs to be done, so it's important to know going in what method your company will be using, and what will be expected of you.

Benefits to turnkey investing

While flipping houses and wholesaling are great options for real estate investing, some investors prefer turnkey investments because it affords them several benefits over doing it all yourself.

Distance: The most obvious benefit that many investors reap from turnkey investments is the ability to invest in a property from a distance, without having to live in the area. It's not always easy to be a landlord, and the challenges that come with that are often made even more difficult when you live several thousand miles away from the property. Many people who live on either coast, or even are located outside the United States, rely on turnkey companies to invest in great markets, like the Midwest, where cash flow tends to be highest.

Insight into the market: Another reason many investors prefer to use turnkey companies over doing everything themselves is that a good turnkey company will know their market, likely far better than an outsider could. As a lone investor, you might be able to do some research into the area and learn about things like crime reports, school system ratings, and price ranges, but those are all just naked numbers without knowledge of the heart of the area, something that good turnkey companies have. They know how the people of an area think and feel about that area: which blocks are popular and why, which area of town is better than another. They'll know what kind of reputations certain businesses and neighborhoods have, and they'll be aware of shifts in the local economy. This kind of knowledge is generally limited to long-time locals of an area, which a good turnkey company should be.

Skilled marketers: Since good turnkey companies might buy, sell, and rent dozens or hundreds of homes and properties per month, they have a lot of experience in marketing those properties, and many more resources than a single investor may have on their own. As well as having many resources, their resources are also varied, and they may use things like radio ads, television ads, billboards, and more, to help drive interested and motivated tenants and sellers to their business. Because of their experience and resources, they may be able to find better deals than you could, as well as be able to get tenants faster than you could.

Experience managing properties: Most people, real estate investors included, are not good managers. However, if you work with a turnkey company, you have someone to help with this. Turnkey companies are generally pretty experienced in dealing with contractors during rehab and general maintenance, as well as tenants. Their experience often allows them to make better decisions than someone lacking that experience would make, as well as cut down on the learning curve experienced by a new investor/manager.

Professional, helpful staff: Unless you'd like to take care of all of the rehab, maintenance and upkeep, and administrative duties that come with being a property manager, a turnkey provider can help. They usually have in-house staff to take care of things like a broken toilet, to answer the phones, and to sign leases with new tenants. If they don't have in-house staff, they will work closely with vendors to provide these services.

Keeping it simple: The final benefit to turnkey investing could be said to be one of the most important: simplicity. No matter which turnkey company you invest with, they all have the same goal: to make the investment easier for you. If you invest in a property on your own, you have to take care of all of the moving parts yourself, which many investors find to be overwhelming. The ideal turnkey company seeks to make the investment simple for you, so all you have to do is receive and write checks. It is for this reason alone that many investors have turned to turnkey investing.

Downsides to turnkey investing

While there are many benefits to investing in turnkey rental properties, there are also downsides, and these are the reasons why many investors stay away from turnkey investments. It's important to be aware of possible downsides and pitfalls of any investment you're thinking of making, and this is no different when considering whether to invest in a turnkey rental property. Here are the two main downsides to turnkey investing:

Trust is required: This is possibly the greatest risk when you choose to invest in a turnkey rental property. You must place a great deal of trust in the provider. Turnkey investors are, as I mentioned earlier in the chapter, generally located far from their investment property. Therefore they must place a great deal of trust in their turnkey company, trusting them to choose a property that will yield a profit, in a desirable location, and find a reliable tenant, as well as manage that tenant. The turnkey company will get paid regardless of whether or not you, as the investor, make any profit off of the property, so it's a great deal of trust that you place in one of these companies to make you money. It is very easy for a turnkey provider to take advantage of an out-of-town investor who is unfamiliar with the area, convincing them to invest in a property in a bad location. There have been many stories told by investors where that situation happened to them, and the property ended up being what's referred to as a "pig in lipstick", one that seemed fine but immediately after investing began to cost the investor a lot of money in repairs and other issues.

Finances: The second downside to turnkey rentals is another great risk: that of money. A turnkey company is a business just like any other, and the driving force behind any business is to make money. They have to turn a profit in order to stay operable, and they will do this several ways. Turnkey companies will often buy properties at a nice discount, and then turn around and sell the investment to you at a higher rate, essentially flipping the property to you, for a high price. After that, they make yet more money by managing the property for you.

This is the catch to turnkey properties. You can't have the simplicity of this kind of investing without paying a premium for it. Either you have simplicity, or you pay less and deal with complications yourself, but either way you pay, whether it's in money or your time. Turnkey companies operate on the idea that people want to simplify their investments, and make a profit off of that desire. That said, as I mentioned before, turnkey companies are very good at marketing, and are very often able to find incredible deals in their area, so even if they're going to make a great profit when they sell the investment to you, you're still often getting a very good deal.

Keep in mind important details

Turnkey investing can be a great option for investors who wish to have a more hands-free investment, those who are located in more expensive markets where they may be unable to find good investments for their budgets, and newer investors who would like some help with the particulars and complications that come along with real estate investing. Turnkey companies have great resources for investors. However, it is very important to be a smart investor. Experts suggest that, even though turnkey investing is a great option for those who are located far away from the property, prospective investors should go check out the property in person, even if that means flying across the country, so that they know what they're investing in.

It's also advisable to know your property manager well. As an investor, you'll be putting a lot of trust into the turnkey company, so it's important that you're on the same page. Some helpful and important things to ask your property manager are:

> "How much experience does your company have?"
>
> "What fees does your company charge?"
>
> "How long, on average, does it take your company to find tenants for new properties?"
>
> "Will your company provide statements each month so I can keep track of expenses and income?"
>
> "What are your company's weaknesses?"
>
> "How well do you know the area?"

Generally, turnkey rental properties are a great form of real estate investing for those investors without the time, interest, or ability to personally renovate and maintain real estate investments. The most important thing to remember about turnkey investments is to do your research and know what you're getting into, and not be blinded by the possible benefits to this kind of investment.

Chapter 6:
Invest in REITs

If you like the sound of real estate investment in theory, but in practice find yourself unable to come up with the credit or cash to purchase an entire property outright, then Real Estate Investment Trusts might be more speed. As mentioned previously, ever since the 1960s when they were created REITs have been investing in different types of properties and letting their shareholders split a majority of the profits based on the percentage of the total based on what each one owns. REITs are tax exempt in exchange for giving back 90 percent of their total profits to the tax holders. Most REITs generate profits from the usage, sales and mortgaging of different types of properties depending on the type of REIT in question. Overall, each REIT must have at least 100 shareholders and no five shareholders can control 50 percent of the total or more.

REIT benefits

Little for you to do: Unlike when you are renting out a property, and thus always have 20 things to do, when you invest in an REIT, all you have to do is choose the right REIT for you, and then assuming you choose wisely, all you have to do is sit back and collect your profits. You don't need to worry about choosing property or maintaining it at all, you just need to find an REIT that is a good choice in the moment and then proceed accordingly.

Less personal risk: Regardless of the REIT you choose, their end goal is to make as much of a reliable profit as possible. To this end they are likely going to employee the best individuals they can to make this goal a reality. This means that as long as you choose wisely up front, then you are likely going to have someone that is much more experienced holding your financial reigns for good or ill, though likely mostly for good. What's more, the cost is going to be much lower than with either purchasing rental property or flipping houses as you only have to put down a fraction of the cost to receive proportionally the same benefits. This means that everyone who invests in a given REIT is due back the same 7 percent return on their investment no matter what proportional to what they first put in.

Less commitment: When it comes to most types of real estate investment, even if everything else goes wrong you still have a property in hand. However, there are certainly going to be moments where this is a negative, not a positive which is when the limited level of ownership inherent in an REIT really shines. You will always be able to determine what your shares of the REIT are worth, and if you see a price that like, you can sell, simple as that.

Best retirement option: The biggest downside to REITs is that the profit that you make on them is taxed twice, severely cutting down on your overall profit if you don't choose to put it into a long term retirement account. However, this naturally makes REITs the best choice when you are looking for these types of investments. What's more, REITs mostly tend to remain quite stable, even when other parts of the market are in a panic. This is because REITs pay out dividends which mean there will always be a point where they are more valuable to keep than to sell, even when the going gets rough.

Equity REITs

An equity REIT is any REIT which is primarily focused on selling, renovating, acquiring or managing a specific type of real estate. They are the most profitable of the REIT types which also makes them the most common type as well. Equity REITS are generally broken down into storage facilities, resorts and hotels, office or industrial, health care, residential and retail and each has different requirements for success depending on the current strength of the local market. This means that if you plan on investing, you are going to need to choose the type of equity REIT that is right for you.

Residential REIT: As the name implies, residential REITs focus on residential property, primarily large apartment complexes. When it comes to choosing a profitable REIT you are going to want to be aware of where the holdings are located and what, if any, construction is scheduled in that area in the near future. These types of construction projects don't come about without lots of meetings which means a good place to start is with local town hall meeting records if you hope to catch up on what is going on.

Retail REIT: Retail REITs focus on retail space and are typically further specialized so they control either shopping malls or shopping centers. Determining if a given REIT in this sector is profitable or not is as easy as visiting their holdings and seeing how many vacancies there currently are. Otherwise, the high cost of building these types of establishments typically keeps new construction, and thus new competition, low.

Office and Industrial REIT: These two REITs are often lumped together because they typically deal in longer, more stable, lease lengths than the previous REITs even though an office REIT wouldn't deal in industrial space directly and vice versa. The strength of these REITs is largely based around what the real estate market was like when the current round of tenants signed their current leases. If the market was full of available properties, then current rates are likely to be below average while if it was low on properties then the current rates are generally going to be higher. Of the two, office REITs are often prone to bigger swings in both directions while industrial REITs are more likely to provide smaller and more reliable returns.

Health care REIT: Health care REITs are one of the most recession proof types of REITs available. They focus on hospital and hospital adjacent buildings, which there is always going to be a demand for, plus new hospital related construction is somewhat rare, limiting competition. You do need to be aware of what the current state of medical payment reimbursement at the federal level is like, however, if it is up then this type of REIT is a good choice, if it is down then this type of REIT is much riskier.

Storage REIT: If you are looking to get into real estate investment for the absolute lowest total cost possible then investing in a local storage REIT is the best place to start. Self-storage is a recession proof business that is currently gaining in popularity in the investment market. Assuming the area that the REIT holdings are in isn't flush with self-storage space then it is hard to lose.

Hotel and Resort REITs: Unlike storage REITs, hotel and resort REITs typically have the highest buy-in and are also going to be hit the hardest by a recession as discretionary travel is always the first to go when hard times appear. The profit margins if things go well are often quite enticing, however, just be sure you know what the overall market is going to be doing while you are investing.

Non-equity REIT types

Mortgage REIT: A mortgage REIT isn't interested in owning or renting out property so much as it is in gathering and profiting from the debt that other people owe on various types of real estate. You can think of owning shares in this type of REIT as something similar to owning a debt portfolio instead.

Hybrid REIT: If you can't decide if you want an equity or a non-equity REIT, then a hybrid REIT is for you. This type of REIT focuses on both owning property and owning debt in equal measure and are a great way to diversify as much as possible.

Choosing an REIT

When it comes time to choose an REIT that you are comfortable with, you are going to once more start by doing your homework. This means visiting the holdings in question if possible and also looking for records related to their historical dividend yields, with 7 percent once again being the target number. You will also need to think about the REITS level of growth for the past few years. This can be done by first looking into their net income and operation funds from which you can determine their year over year cash flow. You are going to want to choose an REIT that has at least a 5 percent average growth range per year.

Another good way to determine if a certain REIT is worth pursuing is by determining what portion of the REIT's shareholders are what are known as institutional investors.

Institutional investors are things like investment firms and the more institutional investors a REIT has, the more likely it is that the investment is going to remain solid in the short as well as the medium term. Last but not least, when it comes time to price out individual shares, you are going to want to focus on REITs that are in your budget, but at the same time are not budget priced. Shares that are priced to move are a sure indication that the REIT that is offering them has either just been through some rough times or that it expects rough times ahead, and either way it is a proposition that you should want no part of.

Chapter 7:
Invest in Properties to Flip

As previously discussed, if you like the idea of working with tangible property, but at the same time don't want to work with the same property forever, then flipping houses directly instead of renting them out might be the best real estate investment choice for you.

Getting Started

First and foremost, you are going to want to take the time to find the right area that ultimate buyers are going to be interested in using the same techniques discussed in chapter 4. This should allow you to have a good idea of what area you want to find a property in as well as what you can realistically expect to get for it once you have fixed it up properly. With this out of the way, your biggest challenge is then going to be waiting for the right property to come along. Waiting for the right property isn't a passive process, however, and will instead have you looking at plenty of different properties and working out the various costs associated with each.

Find your team: Unless you are already a licensed contractor, odds are you won't have the skills required to determine the true cost of a property on your own, especially not your first time out. As such, before you even set foot on a potential investment property you are going to want to ensure that you have a team in place ready to have your back throughout the entire process. While a good team is going to be expensive, they are also going to be worth it and allow you to make much more overall than you otherwise would. Finally, you are going to want to build your team first so that you know how much they are going to cost you when you are working out if a property is going to be worth your time.

When looking for your team, generally you are going to want to stick with individuals who are willing to get paid once things all come together, this is crucial to help you keep from spending money through out of pocket costs. First up, you are going to need to find a real estate agent who specializes in helping individuals flip houses. Typically, this means you are going to want to find an REO agent, which is a real estate agent that specifically specializes in bank foreclosures which are often going to be your bread and butter as a property flipper.

With an agent on board, the next two people you are going to want to find are a real estate attorney as well as a certified public account that specializes exclusively in real estate investment. These two folks are likely going put a premium on their services, but you don't have a choice but to add it to your operating costs and keep moving. In order to ensure that you can flip property as easily and securely as possible, these two individuals are crucial, no ifs ands or buts about it. If you are especially worried about these types of costs, keep in mind that they are in no way standardized which means you should feel free to negotiate as you feel appropriate in an effort to get the best price possible.

Once you have a firm handle on your legal team, you are going to want to then focus on finding the best general contractor that you can, as well as a backup in case the first doesn't work out. While you will always be able to get away with certain projects in a do it yourself fashion, if you try and tackle larger jobs by yourself then you are likely going to end up spending more to fix your mistakes in the long run than you would by simply paying someone to do the job right the first time.

Choosing the right general contractor is essential as you are going to be spending a lot of time with this person and they are more or less going to be in charge of all of the renovations that are planned. This means you are going to want to get local recommendations about contractors, which you can get from local hardware stores if nowhere else. All you need to do is ask about contractors that always by the highest quality products. Finding the right contractor means you won't have to worry about finding a team for remodeling as the contractor should have that covered.

Choose a property

With a team in place you will finally be ready to start looking at properties that seem promising. This means you will want to take your contractor with you to every property so they can help you determine the actual cost that will be required to get the property into show-ready shape. With the contractor on hand you should be able to determine the reasonable costs associated with making repairs to the property as well as what the after repair value (ARV) of the property will be, a major step to determining if a property is actually worth your time. While at a property with your contractor it is important to take your time and to check everything about the property from tip to tail. This means starting with the roof and not stopping until you reach the foundation. You will also want to include an inspection of major systems such as electrical, plumbing and heating/cooling.

When it comes to making a decision on a specific piece of property, you are going to need to keep in mind the fact that the property might not sell as soon as it is finished being remodeled which means you are going to need to factor in additional maintenance fees as well. If you are unsure about the current state of the market in your area, especially if it is currently a deep buyer's market, then you may need to plan on sitting on a property for up to 12 months. If the market in your region is currently anything but strong you are likely going to want to ensure that you have a backup plan as well as a main plan to go along with every investment, just in case.

Paying for a property

After you have found a property that you are willing to take the plunge on, all that is left is to figure out how you are going to pay for it. Even if you don't have enough cash to purchase your property outright, there are still plenty of ways to get control of a property depending on your specific financial circumstances.

Hard money or private money loans: If you have 35 percent of the total cost of a given property, and proof of a profitable ARV, then you may qualify for what are known as hard money or private money loans. These loans are given out by private individuals, generally as a means of creating a passive income. If you want to qualify for one of these types of loans, then you are going to need a 620 credit score as well as an income to debt ratio of 45 percent or less and no bankruptcies or foreclosures for 10 years or more.

You will then see an interest rate of at least 10 percent but as much as 16 percent with extra fees totaling somewhere around 3 percent of what the total amount of the loan is for. They can be approved in as little as two weeks and will require you to submit relevant proof of financial solvency as well as estimates regarding ARV, repair costs and initial costs. These types of loans are particularly useful to new investors as their approval lies more on whether or not the property in question is a good value as opposed to any personal skill involved.

Bank Financing: If your credit score is over 700 and you have a debt coverage ratio that is greater than 1.25 then you may be able to get a loan from a traditional financial institution. These loans will provide up to 65 percent of the total cost of the property, after renovation costs are considered. The rate on this loan is going to be much less than with a hard money loan, as low as 5 percent. Securing bank financing is likely going to take much longer, however and will require tax returns, bank statements, a property appraisal, settlement sheets, repair cost estimates and a purchase contract.

Crowd Funding: If you are looking to raise proceeds to purchase a property for the purpose of flipping it and you don't have the qualifications above, or the time to wait for a traditional loan, then you might find luck crowd funding your real estate loan. Available in as little as three days assuming your pitch is worthwhile, a crowdfunded real estate loan is often good for as much as 85 percent of the total cost of the property in question including repair cost estimates or 65 percent of the total ARV whichever is less. Qualified applicants will be required to have a debt to income ration of under 50 percent as well as a credit score that is at least 600 and a clean history of bankruptcies and foreclosures. Having a successful history of flipping houses will help, though it is not required. The interest rates for these types of loans is anywhere for 9 to 15 percent.

Chapter 8: Staging a Home for Resale

While staging a home or apartment is technically optional during the selling process, it really shouldn't be. The home you're trying to sell is the same as any other commodity: it needs to be marketed. It should be made appealing to the type of person you are trying to sell it to, and if you skimp on this step, you run the risk of ending up with less than your asking price or dealing with a longer marketing period. If you're an investor who makes a living flipping houses, these risks aren't worth the time you'd save skipping the staging.

When you stage a house, what you're really doing it setting it up so that the prospective buyer, when viewing the outside and walking through the home, can see themselves living there. You want them to walk in and think that this is the perfect place for them, to start imagining how they'll decorate this room, or where they'll put that furniture, or the lovely dinner parties they'll have in the kitchen. Staging is the way realtors accomplish this.

The definition of staging is evident in the word itself: it's like setting the stage for a play. Everything should be intentional, pleasing to the eye, inoffensive or obtrusive. You want it to appeal to the type of person you would like to sell it to, and if you're just trying to flip the house, chances are you want it to appeal to many different types of people. There are several ways that realtors stage houses.

Cleaning

Deep clean the house: Possibly the most important step, if not the easiest, is to deep clean the entire house. You want the walls to sparkle, the floors to shine, everything down to the grout should be scrubbed. There shouldn't be dust anywhere, and windows should be gleaming. You want the prospective buyer to walk through and see the house itself and all it has to offer, not the dust on the air vents or the smudges on the fridge. You're trying to sell something, and while buyers obviously know that the house has been lived in, it's not brand new, you want them to feel like it was made just for them.

Declutter: Almost as important as scrubbing the house is decluttering it. Clear counters, tidy bookshelves, and open floor space all serve to open up the house and make it welcoming, while at the same time leaving space for the buyer to envisage their own belongings in the house. If the house is full of nothing but personal knick-knacks, it doesn't allow room for the buyer's imagination. It also detracts from the feature your house has to offer. A buyer is less likely to be excited about the built-in bookshelves in the children's room if the shelves are covered in toys scattered haphazardly around.

Clutter also makes it seem like the house doesn't have enough storage space. After all, if there is space for all of these things to be stored out of sight, why aren't they? Also important to note is that buyers will likely be interested in seeing cabinets and closet spaces, so tossing everything into a closet may not be the best solution. Often an outside storage unit will come into play, or a kind friend or family member's garage.

Make it smell nice: A buyer shouldn't walk into your home and smell your pets, or last night's dinner, or laundry. These things, as well as kids, a mildew bathroom, and garbage disposals can all contribute to a less-than-attractive home smell that you may not even notice. The sense of smell is very closely linked to memory, and when a buyer is later trying to decide between properties, their memory of your home will likely be swayed by the type of scent it had.

There are easy ways to ensure that these memories are good ones. Coating an apple in cinnamon and baking it in the oven gives off a homey vibe reminiscent of the holiday season, which many find to be comforting and warming. Other methods are to pop a tray of slice and bake cookies in the oven, burn a vanilla scented candle, or put a pot of water on to boil with a homemade potpourri of lemon slices, cinnamon sticks, and other aromatics.

Another good tip is to put pieces of lemon into the garbage disposal to help get rid of food odors. You could use disinfectant and scented sprays to rid your home of unwanted odors, but often they leave a more industrial, artificial scent behind, while the tips listed above serve to make the house feel more homey, which is, after all, what staging is about.

If you smoke in the home, try to limit yourself to smoking outside. Making sure all fabrics are freshly washed before an open house also helps to keep the home smelling fresh, as well as ensuring the carpets are clean, though that's a step that should be taken care of when deep cleaning the house.

Decoration

Maximize curb appeal: This may be something you've heard over and over on home decorating shows, but the truth is it's actually very important. Many prospective buyers will drive by a house before ever deciding to do tour or attend an open house, and often they make their decision based solely on how appealing the outside of the house is. Make sure your home makes a good first impression by taking care of the following:

- Ensure the house numbers are large, well-placed, and easy to read

- Plant greenery and blooming flowers

- Repaint or stain the porch, shutters, and other wooden fixtures if needed

- Wash the windows

- Power wash the siding and sidewalks

Another way to make your home appealing on the outside is to turn your front porch into a welcoming space. Put out a clean, attractive door mat, some blooming potted flowers, and if there's room, a piece or two of neat porch furniture. Make sure the porch light works, and leave it on after dark, in case buyers drive by late.

Grouping furniture: Most people believe that rooms feel bigger if the furniture is pushed against the walls, leaving floor space in the middle. That isn't the case. Rather than pushing the furniture away, bring it together in conversational groups in the middle of the room, placing pieces so that the traffic flow of the room is clear. This method of furniture placement makes the room feel more user-friendly, as well as opening up the room. Also give yourself permission to move pieces from room to room. You may have bought that chair for the living room, but that doesn't mean it won't look better in a bedroom as a little sitting area.

Painting and color: A fresh coat of paint throughout the house can do wonders to make it feel open, welcoming, clean, and new. Now is not the time to be creative or show your personality through wall colors, however. Go for neutral tones to make everything look pulled together and sophisticated, as well as providing a blank canvas for a homeowner to be able to envision whatever wall color they would like, rather than your "adventurous" lime green living room wall. Painting is also a great way to make room feel larger. If your kitchen is a bit small, considering painting it the same color as the adjacent dining room, or even the hallway. The seamless look makes the space look bigger. Another trick is to hang curtains the same color as your wall, this also makes the space look bigger.

Paint isn't the only color you should be thinking about when staging a house. Also important are draperies, accent pieces, and bedroom color schemes. Just as with the paint, it's a good idea to go for a neutral color scheme. However, don't be afraid to play with color a bit in more intimate spaces like the bathroom or a bedroom. Painting a single accent wall a darker color, or using darker fabrics on the bed and windows can give the room a more intimate, welcoming feel. For the master bedroom, consider going gender-neutral in the coloring and decorations; you want all buyers to be interested in it and be able to see themselves relaxing in the space.

Decorate: While you want to get rid of clutter, you also want the house to seem able to be lived-in, and this is where decorating comes in. Thoughtfully placed accent pieces or coordinating knick-knacks can do a lot to draw in a buyer and make them want to see more of the house. A good rule is the rule of threes: things in groups of three are pleasing to the eye. Rather than lining up three candlesticks on the coffee table, however, consider varying the pieces in height, grouping them together in the center of the table. Make it look effortless, but polished. For maximum effect, group pieces by color or type. Other elements that will make a home feel welcoming are things like a bowl of fruit on the table or a vase of cut flowers on the kitchen counter.

There are smaller elements that should be paid attention to that you may not notice but a prospective buyer may. In the bathroom, make sure that any towels you may have out are fluffy and clean, not pilling or old. Soaps should be new, mirrors should be cleaned. In the kitchen, an easy way to spruce things up is to replace the front of the cabinets and drawers, as well as the drawer pulls. Be sure to open the windows for at least ten minutes before an open house or tour, so it's not stuffy inside.

Lighting: Proper lighting can make a home feel warm and welcoming. Increase the wattage of bulbs in your lamps and fixtures, aiming for 100 watts per 50 square feet. Vary the type of lighting, not relying on all overhead lights or all lamps. A good way to do this is to make sure that you have three types of lighting: ambient lighting (overhead), task lighting (pendant lights or desk lamps), and accent lighting (on tables and walls). Another way to maximize your home's lighting is to make use of natural light. Open the blinds and curtains, letting sunlight stream in. It makes the house feel more welcoming, as well as more open.

The bottom line when it comes to staging a home for resale as an investor is to strike a balance between spending too much money and not enough. If you skimp, you run the risk of having to settle for less than your asking price, as buyers might not be as taken by your house as they could have been if you'd put in a little more effort. If you spend too much, that's money that's coming out of your pocket, and in the end, making a profit is what investing is about. It's important to set the stage for the sale, and if you take care, you'll find the house will sell itself.

Chapter 9:
Invest in Properties to Wholesale

All told, wholesaling a property requires many of the same skills that you will need to possess if you hope to flip a property successfully. What's more, you don't need contractor skills or a full team, though you will still likely be making less on each individual transaction due to the nature of the process. In return, you don't need to actually do any work to the properties you find, all you need is the vision to spot a diamond in the rough when you see one and be able to convince someone else to share that vision with you. Specifically, you take the time to find properties that can afford for you to make a little on top of what the property flipper is going to make, get the great deal in writing and then sell the property to someone you have already found who is into that type of thing.

Before you get out there and start looking for supremely undervalued properties, the first thing you are going to need to do is to determine what the regulations in your state have to say about property wholesaling. Lots of states view property wholesaling in different ways, and some states don't allow it in its traditional form unless you have a real estate license. If you find out that you are in one of these supremely limiting states, then you are going to instead want to participate in what is known as a double close whereby you close on the property a few days before you close on selling the property. What matters most is that you take the time to find a real estate lawyer and have them explain to you the specifics of what is and is not allowed in the state that you reside in.

Find the right prices

When it comes to finding the right properties to sell, you are going to need to be even more creative than if you are looking for properties to flip in the traditional sense. This is because you need to be able to get a property at such a price that you can squeeze in at least $5,000 for yourself on top of everything else to ensure that you make the process worth your time. In this case you are likely going to want to ignore posted listings almost entirely as they are likely going to already be filled out in such a way that there is little extra to be made in terms of additional profit.

Instead you are going to want to get to individuals who might be planning on selling, or find themselves in a situation where they don't have a choice but to sell as they will not only be more agreeable to a price you can actually work with, but they will not have yet contacted a real estate agent which will makes things easier for you still. For starters you can simply drive around in areas that you know could produce profitable properties, and look for signs of people getting ready to move out. Finding a property at this point is likely going to be your best chance to jump on it early and you are going to want to take full advantage of it.

If visual surveillance doesn't lead to any hits, you next step should be to look for debt collection lists in your area that are available for sale. There are numerous websites that contain this sort of information for every area of the country and a quick online search should easily reveal those in an area near you. Once you have this information, the best way to take advantage of it is sure to surprise you. Specifically, if you are looking to maximize results as compared to costs then you are going to want to contact the individuals whose information you purchased via a direct mailing campaign. Overall, the rate of return is about 3 percent of the total, with costs at roughly 40 cents per unit. This means that for 400 you can reasonably expect 30 people to contact you. From there you can expect about a 10 percent success rate which means you might get three successful properties in the bargain. While this might not sound like much on its face, in reality this could easily be more than $20,000 in profit, which isn't a bad return on 400.

Know the right offer

After you have located a property that seems as though you can make a profit on it, you will then want to determine what the MAO, maximum allowed offer, is going to be if you hope to cash in on your finder's fee. Determining the MAO is easy, you simply start with the ARV and subtract from it the profit the flipper will want to make, the estimated repair costs and any other costs that are going to be factored into the total. Whatever is left over is what you as the wholesaler can expect to make on the endeavor.

While you will likely find that you need help determining these numbers at first, over time you will discover you are able to accurately estimate repairs in the same way that a contractor would, by individual job components. For starters, however you can work out what the average ARV in an area is online and then go from there. Once you know what your MAO is going to be, you are ready to try and get the best deal on the property possible via a vigorous round of negotiation.

Vigorous round of negotiation

If you hope to make money as a property wholesaler, then you are going to be living and dying by your negotiation skills more often than you might at first be comfortable with. Negotiation is a skill, however, which means that it will only get better with practice. Alternatively, you may find that you can negotiate more easily if you think of it less as something negative and more as something collaborative.

Regardless, all successful negotiation can be broken up into three parts: process, behavior and substance. Process is the way in which you approach a given negotiation, and a confident process can do wonders when it comes to effective negotiations. Substance can be thought of as the details at the heart of the negotiation, and your process should ensure the substance goes in your favor as well. Finally, you can think of the interaction between you and the other party as the behavior of the negotiation. Keep this in mind and consider the following tips to ensure every real estate negotiation ends, if not in your favor, at least on terms that you find acceptable.

1. When it comes to submitting an offer, you are going to always want to meet with the other party directly if possible. Assuming the market is in your favor, then you are going to have most of the power going into the negotiation and the best way to capitalize on that power is to meet the other person face to face. Alternatively, if the market is currently in the other party's favor you are going to want to negotiate via email instead as this will balance out the power disparity somewhat.

2. When you do meet the other person face to face, you are going to want to submit your offer and them remain completely silent, no matter how long it takes. If the other party also appears to be dead set on not saying anything either, after 90 seconds you can repeat your offer once more. This will limit the other party significantly in terms of how they can proceed, firmly establishing your power in the negotiation even more.

3. Another reason that you will want to hold the negotiations in person as long as the conditions are favorable is that you can learn a lot about the other person via their body language. A counter offer that is submitted using open body language indicates that the other party is willing to reach a consensus, while closed body language indicates that they did not like your original offer at all and timid body language indicates that they have no strength in their currently expressed convictions.

4. You will want to keep the current state of the market in mind at all times, and not just to determine the best way to hold the negotiation. If the market is in the buyer's favor, then you are going to be able to more easily make additional demands without worrying about the whole thing falling through. Additionally, you can take 10 percent off of the top of your offering price while also request that the seller pay the closing costs. Alternatively, if it is currently a seller's market then you are going to need to be prepared to make a little bit less on the deal overall and also be willing to pay the asking price, depending on the overall quality of the property. If the market is in the seller's favor, then you will do far better with quantity than you will with individual payout quality.

Finishing up

After you have successfully negotiated a property sale price that you can profit from in one way or another, all that is left to do is to turn around and sell the contract to someone who will actually do something with it. Finding a house flipper that you can work with on the long term is extremely beneficial for everyone involved. The flipper will get a steady stream of houses to profit from and you won't even need to find more than one person to complete your wholesales.

When it comes to finding someone to reliably purchase your properties, you are going to want to go with a flipper who has access to cash or at least a hard money loan. While it might seem like it would be difficult to find these individuals, you can often find likely candidates by checking out a local real estate investment club and asking around for the right type of buyers.

Conclusion

Thank for making it through to the end of *Real Estate Investing: Comprehensive Beginner's Guide for Newbies,* let's hope it was informative and able to provide you with all of the tools you need to achieve your goals both in the near term and for the months and years ahead. Remember, just because you've finished this book doesn't mean there is nothing left to learn on the topic. Becoming an expert at something is a marathon, not a sprint.

The next step is to stop reading already and to get to work deciding which type of real estate investment is right for you, right now. While you may be tempted to try out more than one at a time, a better choice would be to instead focus on establishing a reliable income stream from one type of investment before moving onto the next. Especially early on, splitting your focus can easily mean splitting your chance for success.

Please check out our Amazon Author Page to find selections like this!

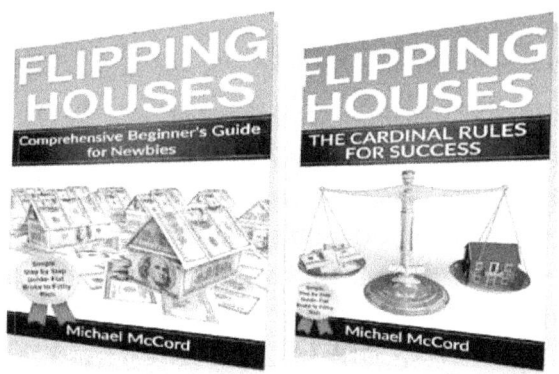

https://www.amazon.com/Flipping-Houses-Comprehensive-Beginners-Properties-ebook/dp/B01MQCR3OP

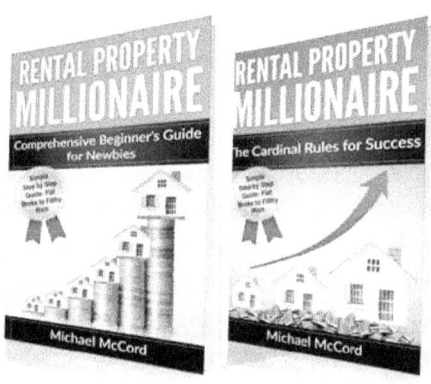

https://www.amazon.com/Rental-Property-Investing-Comprehensive-Investment-ebook/dp/B01M69Y22J

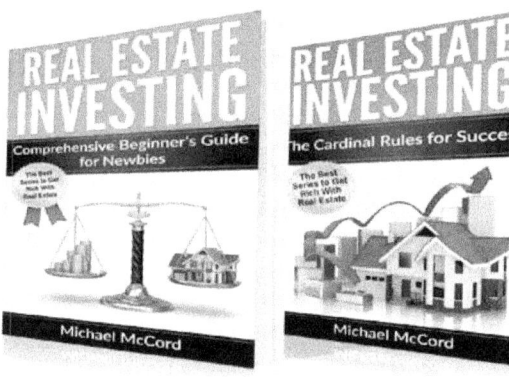

https://www.amazon.com/Real-Estate-Investing-Comprehensive-Beginners-ebook/dp/B01MQ0VTIU

https://www.amazon.com/Real-Estate-Agent-Comprehensive-Generating-ebook/dp/B01M72UKYO

https://www.amazon.com/Rental-Property-Investing-Comprehensive-Beginners-ebook/dp/B01LI5L6R6

Last but certainly not least, if you found this book useful in anyway, a review on Amazon is always appreciated! You can write a review on our book's page which you can access here:

https://www.amazon.com/Real-Estate-Investing-Comprehensive-Beginners-ebook/dp/B01LWIK3V2/

www.ingramcontent.com/pod-product-compliance
Lightning Source LLC
Chambersburg PA
CBHW060419190526
45169CB00002B/974